Crush (ed)

OrangeBooks Publication

Smriti Nagar, Bhilai, Chhattisgarh - 490020

Website: **www.orangebooks.in**

© Copyright, 2023, Author

All rights reserved. No part of this book may be reproduced, stored in a retrieval system, or transmitted, in any form by any means, electronic, mechanical, magnetic, optical, chemical, manual, photocopying, recording or otherwise, without the prior written consent of its writer.

Crush(ed)

A Collection of Poetry

Russhveen Ubann

OrangeBooks Publication
www.orangebooks.in

ABOUT THE BOOK

Read it again if you think this is just poetry.

There are two kinds of love

One that you always give.

One that you never receive.

1

*They didn't own each
other so the fear of
falling was sweeter,
much larger than the fear
of losing one another.*

2

*She wanted to wake up to
his fragrance every day,
waking up to his memories
wasn't bad either.*

3

He was slipping through her fingers even though she had been holding him firmly, please don't leave yet, She whispered, I wanna hold you more tightly.

4

*Every day she kept
listening to everything
he didn't say.*

5

The pain tells where the heart is.

6

They kill you brutally and then ask you to live happily.

7

And the moment you will realize how you made her feel your heart will start to bleed.

8

*She was never silent,
she was hurt.*

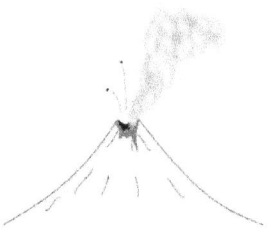

9

One day she finally got to see his eyes full of love but for someone else.

10

*Sadness comes out at night,
it always will.*

11

She rested her head on his shoulder and asked, What if you'll never find a lover like me?

12

*She smelled a lot like
love and heartbreak.*

13

*Even though he stabbed her heart
a million times, it was still smiling.*

14

A garden full of roses but all he chose to see was thorns.

15

She was a broken wine glass in a secret garden.

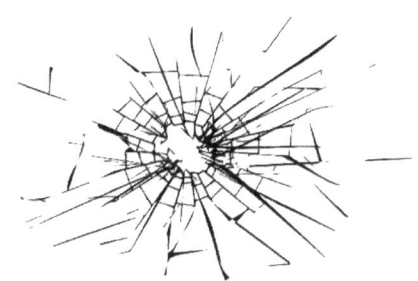

16

They lie, secrets don't last forever else he would have.

17

She wished she was brave enough to free the both of them at the right time.

18

She was a fabulous book but he wasn't a much of a reader.

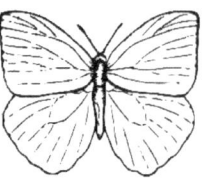

19

*He reminded her of lost love, mugs
with half coffee and
 empty wine bottles.*

20

He kept burning her heart everyday but she never stopped playing with the ashes.

21

She didn't know who was more stubborn that night, the rain or her tears.

22

*He was colder than
that chilly night, her
soul is still shivering.*

23

*How easily he turned into
everything he said he wouldn't.*

24

And when he left, he asked her to do the most difficult thing, he asked her to stay happy.

25

*He said he didn't miss her
and then,
she saw his eyes.*

26

That night, she heard a stranger in his voice.

27

*She didn't know who was crying
louder the night he left,
she or the sky.*

28

*Her heart was drenched
with tears and he was
the only umbrella
she ever wanted.*

29

She swore on those falling tears, "you'll never see me again".

30

How beautifully we build our houses in their hearts just for someone else to live in it.

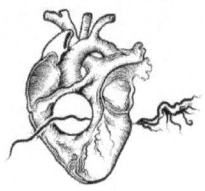

31

She was standing right at the edge and he pushed her.

32

She could melt the stones but not his heart.

33

The day she'll count all the stars in the sky will be the day she'll stop loving him.

34

The same rain that looked so
beautiful, drowned her.

35

No one told her, she will have to meet more tears and less dreams at night.

36

*Drowning in this ocean till
she managed to survive.*

37

*She thought the story was
about her, little did she
know she was just a part
of his story.*

38

They were just two mistakes meant to be.

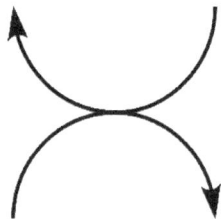

39

She became the moon in order to be with him throughout his darkness.

40

*He owed her sleep,
lots of sleep.*

41

*The way she loved him
unconditionally,
 was truly magical.*

42

Gone are the days when people fell in love with the souls and not faces.

43

She wished she never knew what she felt for him.

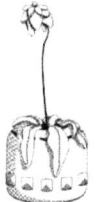

44

*He was the perfect
example of what
she could never have.*

45

*He was the poem which
she was never
able to complete.*

46

He was her favorite heartbreaker.

47

He reminded her of fresh coffee beans, smooth whiskey, unrequited love and last heartbreak.

48

You don't know how hurt you are until you breakdown in the middle of your sleep.

49

*Everything she was
afraid of
happening, happened.*

50

*And if loving him means
staying away,
She swore, she will vanish.*

51

*She didn't know
what was harder,
reminding herself or
convincing herself
every morning that
he has gone.*

52

Never feared the word "end" till he did it.

53

Unfortunately, he didn't want to be the happiest guy on this planet.

54

*It killed her to the point
where she could no
longer bleed.*

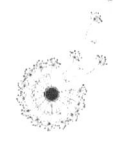

55

She made a wish and 'he' didn't come true.

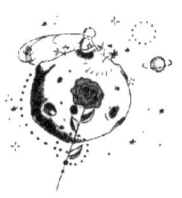

56

*Not everyone is
interested in reading
the entire book,
they'll flip through*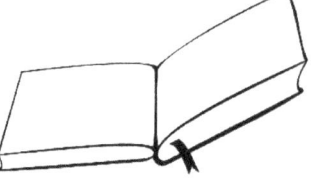
the pages and will bookmark you there forever.

57

And she slowly smelled like burnt roses.

58

What a beautiful flower she was until slowly and slowly someone plucked all its petals.

59

*She continued loving him even though
he promised to leave.*

60

*And when he was going down the flames,
she was burning with him.*

61

He was her favorite sad song, Silence was the only lyrics it had.

62

She wasn't the home he was looking for.

He wanted to wander in shelters.

63

She was addicted to the turbulence he bought to her, It made her feel alive.

64

She wrote the last letter which said,

"And when I leave, I will leave you like I never loved you,

I will be there for you when everyone else will give up on you,

I will listen to you when you won't be able to listen to your own thoughts,

And when you will feel numb, I will hug you and remind you what a human touch feels like".

Crush (ed)

*I will hold your hand until you forget
what tears are,*

*But when I leave, you will miss me and the way
I could bring you back to the life,*

You will miss the fireworks within you,

You will miss being sane,

You will look for me in the sky,

And when I leave, when I leave,

I will take a piece of you with me".

ABOUT THE AUTHOR

I am currently growing like the phases of the moon where my final destination is the Full Moon.

ACKNOWLEDGEMENT

*Thank you dear memories, tears
and reality checks,*

*Without you I wouldn't have been the person
I am today.*

Thank you Moon for never giving up on me.

*Biggest thank you to my cheerleader, supporter,
personal diary and,*

*And my Big B, Sahej. Without you, the heart
would have been full and these,*

Pages would have been empty.

Author, because of you, for you.

*"Oh but,
The Full Moon will always
remind you of me."*

www.ingramcontent.com/pod-product-compliance
Lightning Source LLC
LaVergne TN
LVHW061600070526
838199LV00077B/7124